UNITED STATES CHRISTIAN COMMISSION

FACTS,

PRINCIPLES, AND PROGRESS.

JANUARY, 1864.

PHILADELPHIA:
WILLIAM S. & ALFRED MARTIEN,
No. 606 Chestnut Street.
1864.

CONTENTS.

OFFICIAL SANCTION.

From President Lincoln.

EXECUTIVE MANSION,
WASHINGTON, December 12, 1861.

MY DEAR SIR:

Your letter of the 11th inst., and accompanying plan, both of which are returned as a convenient mode of connecting this with them, have just been received. Your Christian and benevolent undertaking for the benefit of the soldiers, is too obviously proper and praiseworthy to admit any difference of opinion. I sincerely hope your plan may be as successful in execution as it is just and generous in conception.

Your obedient servant,

ABRAHAM LINCOLN.

GEO. H. STUART, Esq., Chairman U. S. Christian Commission, Philadelphia.

From the Secretary of War.

MEMORANDUM OF HON. E. M. STANTON.

WASHINGTON CITY, January 24, 1863.

Bishop Janes is authorized to state, that he has received assurance from the Secretary of War, that every facility consistent with the exigencies of the service will be afforded to the Christian Commission, for the performance of their religious and benevolent purposes in the armies of the

United States, and in the forts, garrisons, camps, and military posts.

From the Secretary of the Navy.

NAVY DEPARTMENT, December 16, 1861.

SIR:

I have received your letter of the 11th inst., asking an expression of the Department as to the objects of the United States Christian Commission, to promote the welfare of the soldiers, sailors, marines, &c.

The Department will be gratified with any legitimate means to promote the welfare, present and future, of all who are in the service.

I am, very respectfully,

Your obedient servant,

GIDEON WELLES.

Mr. GEO. H. STUART, Chairman U. S. Christian Commission, Philadelphia.

From the Postmaster-General.

WASHINGTON, January 5, 1863.

DEAR SIR:

The Christian Commission, of which you are chairman, have in hand a noble work, and are performing it, I am well assured, as only a labor of love can be performed.

Yours, respectfully,

M. BLAIR.

To GEO. H. STUART, Chairman U. S. Christian Commission, Philadelphia.

General Meade to ehe United States Christian Commission.

HEADQUARTERS ARMY OF THE POTOMAC,
August 5, 1868.

GEORGE H. STUART, Chairman United States Christian Commission,
13 Bank Street, Philadelphia.

DEAR SIR:

I received recently, through the hands of Mr. Cole, your kind letter of the 27th ult. It will afford me very great pleasure to render you every encouragement and facility in my power to prosecute the good and holy work you have entered upon.

I assure you, no one looks with more favor upon the true Christian, who ministers to the spiritual wants of the dying, or the physical wants of the wounded, than those who are most instrumental in the line of their duty in causing this suffering; hence, you may rest satisfied that in this army your agents and assistants will receive every co-operation, and be treated with all the consideration due the important and noble work they are engaged upon.

I shall be glad to hear from you whenever anything occurs requiring my action, and shall always be ready, as far as the exigencies of the service and my authority will permit, to comply with your wishes.

Very respectfully and truly yours,

GEO. G. MEADE,
Major-General Commanding.

Surgeon-General Hammond to the United States Christian Commission.

SURGEON-GENERAL'S OFFICE,
Washington, D. C., July 20, 1863.

DEAR SIR:

I beg that you will accept my most heartfelt thanks for the devotion to the service of the sick and wounded soldiers at Gettysburg, manifested by the Christian Commission and its agents.

Owing to the military necessities of the occasion, the suffering would have been much greater than it was, but for the aid afforded the medical officers by the benevolent individuals who came to their assistance.

I trust you will convey my thanks to those of your body who acted with the Medical Department at Gettysburg, and assure them how highly I value their labors. Begging you to accept my warmest acknowledgments for your own service in the cause of humanity,

Believe me yours sincerely,

WILLIAM A. HAMMOND,
Surgeon-General.

GEORGE H. STUART, ESQ.,
Chairman U. S. Christian Commission,
Philadelphia, Pa.

U. S. CHRISTIAN COMMISSION.

ORIGIN.

The United States Christian Commission originated at a Convention of Young Men's Christian Associations of the loyal States, called for the purpose, November 16, 1861, in the city of New York.

AIM.

Its object is to promote the spiritual and temporal welfare of the brave men in arms to put down a wicked rebellion.

COMPREHENSIVENESS.

As indicated by its name, the Commission is both *National* and *Christian.*

Like the Government, it embraces all the States, and ministers with impartial hand to our national forces, military and naval, without local or State distinction; and like the Great Founder of Christianity, it embraces both body and soul in the scope of its beneficence.

SPECIALITIES.

Regarding our brave men as *warriors* exposed to the perils of battle, the Commission gives the help that saves life in the day of extremity, and relieves anguish on the field and in the hospital.

Regarding them as *mortal, yet immortal*, it brings to them the light of life in death, and affords Christian burial to the body, when the soul has gone to the spirit-world.

Looking upon them as *citizen soldiers*, only for a time engaged in the pursuits of war, exposed to temptations peculiar to the camp, and in danger of corruption, the Commission brings to bear upon them influences to keep them pure against the day of their return to civil life.

Looking upon them as our *national defence*, and, under God, our *sole dependence* to save the Union, and put down the rebellion, the Commission cheers and strengthens them for duty, and for complete success.

Viewing them as absent members of *Christian homes* and *Christian communities*, the Commission supplies to them in their absence, as well as possible, imperfectly at best, the place of father, mother, brother, sister, wife, and friend, minister and church, to cheer and sustain them in their hardships, toils and perils, temptations and privations.

And esteeming them, above all, as those for whom the Redeemer tasted death, and to whom he sends the message of life eternal, amongst whom there is opportunity for hopeful labor, unparalleled in the past, and never again perhaps to offer in the future, the Commission sends the living Christian teacher, and the printed truth, in hope and confidence of glorious fruit.

AGENCIES FOR THE FIELD.

These are three—MEN, STORES, and PUBLICATIONS.

1. MEN.

Christian ministers and laymen, enlisted as unpaid volunteers, and sent as delegates to battle-fields, hospitals, and camps, form the first great distinctive feature and principal reliance of the Christian Commission.

One, two, or more of these delegates, tried and proven in their adaptations to the work, are retained in each army, as Field Agents, (one as General Field Agent,) to superintend and direct the work, establish stations, obtain facilities, order stores and publications, procure subsistence, and report to the Commission the work done by delegates.

2. Stores.

For distribution by the delegates—that is to say, the distribution of stores by the delegates—is another most important feature of the plans and operations of the Commission.

Without stores to use at the right moment, under direction of the surgeon, the delegate could do little to aid the surgeon in saving life or relieving anguish. He would be paralyzed. But combining the two—delegates and stores—sending trustworthy, kind Christian men to distribute stores, under direction of the surgeons, and to aid them with warm hearts and willing hands filled full of the needful stores,—this is the plan for saving life and relieving misery.

The distribution of stores opens the hearts of those who receive them, to the glad reception of the Gospel, from the lips of delegates who dispense them. It touches the soldiers' hearts, too, with gratitude to the people at home, who send the stores, and keeps alive the bonds of affection between the two.

This plan gives assurance to the generous donors, that the stores they contribute will safely reach the men for whom they are designed. The delegates who distribute the stores are the chosen representatives of the people themselves who give them—men who go, without pay, to labor and suffer, if need be; inspired by the same noble desire as that of the donors themselves,—to relieve and save our suffering heroes.

3. Publications.

The Government furnish none. Chaplains are thrown upon their own resources for religious reading matter to distribute to their men. Many regiments are without chaplains.

The Christian Commission, with its one head and all-embracing plans, is capable of expansion as a distributing agency, for the supply of the entire army and navy with the Scriptures, books, papers, and tracts; and these publications are a power in the hands of delegates, enabling them to cheer and aid faithful chaplains in their work, by filling their hands with means of good, and adding also to the personal influence of the delegates themselves, the power of the press through all the ranks of our national forces.

AGENCIES AT HOME.

Besides the General Executive Committee and its Central Office in Philadelphia, under direction of the Chairman, aided by the Secretary, there are Army Committees of Young Men's Christian Associations in some places, as in Philadelphia, Boston, Washington, Buffalo, Chicago, Peoria, and St. Louis, and in others, branches formed by the Commission itself, as in New York, Baltimore, Pittsburgh, Detroit, and Cincinnati; and also local committees appointed by the people, and recognized by the Commission.

These all coöperate in gathering stores and collecting money to carry on the work in the field.

Returned delegates, full of the facts and fire of the work in the army, on the battle-field, and in the hospitals, act as voluntary agents at home, to enlist other good men to go as delegates, and in collecting money and stores for the work.

Ladies also, in various orgranizations, as Ladies' Aid Societies and Ladies' Christian Commissions, render most efficient service in the home-field—the field of supply.

FACILITIES.

The Government not only recognizes and commends the Christian Commission, but cheerfully grants free transportation of men and supplies over all military railways and upon all Government transports, and gives freely every facility, limited only by absolute military necessities.

Railways almost all generously grant free passes, under proper regulations, for all delegates of the Commission, and transportation of supplies either entirely free or at greatly reduced rates.

Telegraph companies generally, transmit all despatches on business of the Commission without charge.

Military and medical officers afford all information and every opportunity consistently in their power, to enable the Commission to pursue its work intelligently and with success.

ECONOMY.

Work in the field by delegates without salary.

Collections at home by committees and delegates without pay.

Travel and transportation from home to the field, and from the field home again, free.

Telegraphic despatches sent and received without charge.

Tents, ambulances, and railroad transportation within army lines, given by the Government.

Stores in vast quantities made up and sent in freely by the ladies.

Bibles and Testaments furnished gratuitously and abundantly by the American Bible Society.

Offices and store-rooms in most places afforded without charge for rent.

The chief executive work almost everywhere done by men of business without pecuniary reward.

These are the unparalleled economic advantages enjoyed by the Christian Commission for the prosecution of its work.

RESULTS.

General Summary to January 1, 1864.

Cash received at the Central Office and Branch Offices	$398,399.58
Value of Stores donated, ...	527,979.07
Value of Scriptures contributed by American Bible Society, ...	55,327.50
Value of Scriptures contributed by British and Foreign Bible Society, ...	1,677.79
Value of Railroad facilities contributed, . . .	57,890.00
Value of Telegraph facilities contributed, . .	13,040.00
Value of Delegates' services, ...	93,780.00
	$1,148,093,94

Number of Delegates sent, ...	1,563
Copies of Scripture distributed, ...	568,275
Hymn and Psalm Books distributed, ...	502,556
Knapsack Books distributed, ...	1,370,348
Library Books distributed, ...	43,163
Magazines and Pamphlets distributed, . . .	155,145
Religious Newspapers distributed, ...	3,316,250
Pages of Tracts distributed, ...	22,930,428
Silent Comforters distributed, ...	4,115
Boxes shipped to Field or distributed at Home, .	16,339

These figures show something of the work of distribution, the generosity of the people, and the self-sacrificing spirit of the noble men who have volunteered their services, but they do not give the results in saving life, relieving misery, cheering men to duty, and leading them to the Saviour.

It has been repeatedly stated as the calm conviction of surgeons and others conversant with the circumstances at Gettysburg, and witnesses of what was done by delegates of the Commission, that the stores they distributed, besides an untold amount of suffering relieved, more than a thousand lives were saved by them, and on that field alone. What, then, must the results have been of the work of the whole thousand and more, on all fields and in all armies? Who shall tell the joy in thousands of households over these saved ones? Who will estimate the consolations afforded the friends of those who died, by the transmission of their dying messages and tokens of remembrance to them? Who will count the number won to Jesus, and the joy in heaven over their salvation? Some of our commanders know well, and tell in glowing words, the influence of the Commission on their men, to steady them and inspire them with the courage that faces death, and the endurance that wins the victory.

NECESSITIES.

The Government is wisely filling up the ranks of our thinned armies everywhere. New strength is accumulating to be hurled against the rebellion, with plans improved and skill perfected.

The Commission ought also to extend its plans and perfect its operations, so as to meet more fully than ever before the wants of our national forces.

With MEN and MEANS this can be done. There can be the permanent organization of a corps of delegates in each army corps, or its equivalent, provided with tents, stores, publications, and means of transportation, to move when the army moves, and be present with the needed stores, to give the surgeons their personal assistance in every battle;

the nucleus, with which delegates sent as minute men, especially for battle-field work, may combine, and become practically of greater value.

This, however, will require say three hundred delegates in the regular army work, always in the field; more than double the number heretofore engaged, aside from minute men.

MEN, therefore, are needed. Good men, strong men, men of three classes, first rate in each.

1st. Preachers who have head, heart, and lungs to command audience in the open air.

2d. Workers who can distribute wisely, help dress wounds, wash and dress helpless men, make soup and give it, speak to soldiers about salvation, pray with the dying, write letters for them, or do anything the varying circumstances demand.

3d. Business men, to manage affairs at offices and stations, obtain facilities and papers, and direct the work as field agents.

Men of these three classes ARE A FIRST NECESSITY. Let this be marked especially by ministers and working Christians of all denominations, and let them volunteer.

STORES and PUBLICATIONS will be needed in proportion, twice as much as heretofore.

And MONEY in still larger measure.

The purchase of well-selected Field Hospital Libraries will form a new item of cash expenditure, necessarily large, if the want is met.

The purchase of tents, teams, and wagons, indispensable to the proposed corps organization of delegates in the various army corps, is another new and large line of investment requiring money.

This, in addition to the purchase of at least double the amount heretofore required as supplies for distribution, creates necessities which must be met by corresponding liberality on the part of those who supply the sinews of the work.

TO MEET THESE NECESSITIES,

1. Delegates returned, ministers of all denominations, and friends in general of the Commission, are authorized and urged to form committees of three, five, or more in every locality where needed, and report their names for recognition and enrolment to the General Office in Philadelphia, or the District Office nearest to the Committee.

2. All Committees are requested to enlist and recommend to the general officers of the Commission, one, two, or more of the very best men for the work in their community, to go as delegates for the regular term of six weeks or more in the regular army work.

3. All returned delegates, ministers, friends, and committees, are urged to secure and forward stores and money to the General Office or the District Office nearest them.

4. The ladies everywhere are invited to form Ladies' Christian Commissions if they choose, or if already organized under other names, then they are requested to cooperate with the Commission, and in every suitable way aid in the supply of men, money, and stores for the prosecution of its work upon the enlarged scale proposed.

5. Churches are requested to hold monthly meetings of prayer for the soldiers and sailors, and make monthly contributions in aid of the work of the Commission amongst them.

DELEGATE WORK.

NATURE OF THE WORK.

Battle-field Work differs in some respects essentially from army work. Care for the body is first on the battle-field, while in the army the great aim is to save the soul. On the battle-field, life-saving and the relief of hunger, thirst, and pain, strain every nerve and muscle. In the army, talent, energy, and enterprise are tasked in public preaching, private teaching, social meetings, and the distribution of printed truth.

Army Work affords rare opportunities for promoting correspondence between the soldiers and their friends at home, of benefitting them in health and spirits, and unparalleled advantages for preaching the gospel to them, and winning them to the Saviour. It is arranged as follows:

The general field agent selects various army centres convenient both as positions from which to reach surrounding sections of the army, and as places of assembly for the soldiers who may desire to attend religious services. Six, eight, or more of these stations may be established in each army while at rest; and at each station, store, subsistence, and chapel tents are set up, supplied, and manned.

At these stations daily religious services are held. At some of them, two services a day, one social and the other preaching, and from them Bibles, Testaments, and religious publications are supplied to chaplains, and other good men, in such regiments as have those who will take the pains to come in for them, and make the proper distribution. And from these stations, also, delegates go out canvassing, supplying, cheering, benefitting the soldiers, regiment by regiment, and hospital by hospital, through all the army.

In all regiments and hospitals having chaplains, delegates report to the chaplains, and offer them such reading matter for distribution as they may have at command, and render such service in aid of the chaplains, if desired, as they may have time to render. *In all cases the chaplains are to be strengthened, not weakened, and assisted, not hindered, in meeting the responsibilities of their position.*

BATTLE-FIELD WORK.

A battle-field may be as follows, or something like it. In length say ten miles, and five in breadth. Lengthwise from end to end, the two opposing lines of battle are formed a mile or two apart. The battle begins as an artillery duel. Men fall along both lines, and are carried back. The surgeons of each army corps select a point conveniently in the rear for their own wounded men. Thus five, six, or more corps hospitals are formed in an irregular line at wide intervals apart in the rear of each army. As the battle proceeds, one of the contending armies, in advancing line or solid column, assaults the other, and either succeeds or is repulsed, when the intermediate space between the two lines becomes the scene of terrific carnage. The tide of battle may sway from line to line until one or the other yields at last, and is driven back or routed, when carnage is extended as far as the victors pursue the vanquished. Over all this field lie strewn the dead and wounded. Those who can crawl, hobble, or walk, seek shelter in some house or barn, or make their way to the hospitals of their own army corps, whilst others must lie and suffer hunger, thirst, and anguish, until taken up and carried on stretchers or in ambulances to the hospital.

Thus the field. Delegate work on the field is arranged as follows:

All is under direction of a general field agent. He selects a place central to the general field for headquarters. There a store is secured, or two if needed, (or tents are pitched,) and placed in charge of a delegate, who acts as agent, with one, two, or more to assist him in receiving and opening stores, and giving them out to the proper persons. The delegation is divided into committees, each having its own chairman or captain, and a corps hospital is assigned to each committee. The committees, each for itself, pitch tent and open out central to the tents of the several hospitals to which they are assigned, and from thence seek supplies from Commission headquarters at the general station for their work.

This the arrangement. The work begins while the battle rages. The delegate, under direction of the surgeon—for, whatever is done for the wounded or sick, must, in every possible instance, be done under the direction of the surgeon—assists in gathering the wounded from the field, even under the guns of the enemy if need be, and at the hospitals assists the surgeons at the amputating table, or strips off the bloody garments from the mangled men, washes them, and puts clean clothes upon them, or prepares and gives food or drink to them, as the case may be.

When the conflict is over, then comes the work of saving life abroad upon the field, by seeking out and ministering to men in extremity, and also in the hospitals, where gathering thousands need timely service, or they must die.

This, with receiving messages from the suffering heroes, and writing for them to their friends, directing them to the Great Physician, giving Christian burial to the dead, and such religious services as the circumstances will permit, is the general delegate work on the battle-field.

This in brief is the work of delegates.

The term of service is, for battle-field work, two weeks or the emergency; for the army work, six weeks or over.

PERSONAL OUTFIT.

This should be very simple. A respectable suit, with a few shirts, collars, and socks, will be better than any more elaborate outfit to be taken from home. A blanket, and strap, and haversack are furnished by the Commission.

SUPPLIES FOR DISTRIBUTION.

Bibles, Testaments, soldiers' books, papers, and tracts, with stores, are provided by the Commission in the field at each station for gratuitous distribution.

TERMS AND EXPENSE MONEY.

Delegates receive *no pay* for their services, but their expenses are borne by the Commission.

Money for expenses, if need be, is advanced, and the Commission has subsistence arrangements for delegates at all stations made by field agents.

Application can be made in person or by letter at the Central Office, 11 Bank Street, Philadelphia; or to C. Demond, 4 Court Street, Boston; or to N. Bishop, 30 Bible House, New York; or to Joseph Albree, 71 Wood Street, Pittsburgh; or W. T. Perkins, 17 West Third Street, Cincinnati; E. D. Jones, at Exchange Bank, St. Louis; J. V. Farwell, Chicago; William Reynolds, Peoria; Dr. J. D. Hill, Buffalo; O. D. Grosvenor, Rochester, N. Y.; Charles F. Clark, Detroit, Michigan; or to any committee of the Christian Commission in any other place.

HINTS TO COMMITTEES AND OTHERS ABOUT DELEGATES.

From all this it will be seen that *three classes of talent* and adaptation are required in the delegate work—*Preaching*, *Business*, and *Working*.

The enlistment of ministers who can command audience in the open air, of rank and file, is of first importance.

Next, perhaps, and quite as indispensable, is it to secure those who have a knowledge of the world, experience in business, and ability in affairs.

Scarcely less in value are the services of those who are adapted to interest and benefit others in social meetings and personal intercourse.

Four things are indispensable in all—piety and patriotism, good common sense and energy.

Men who do not succeed elsewhere should never be sent to the army, for they will surely fail.

None should be accepted who desire to visit the army or a battle-field for any purpose whatever aside from the work of the Commission.

No matter what the position and ability of the man may be, or how worthy the object he has in view, if he does not wish to put himself under direction of the Commission and its field agents, and make it his paramount business to do the proper work of the Commission, he should not be sent as a delegate.

It is right and proper to aid all worthy men in worthy objects, by letters or otherwise, but the name and facilities of the Commission are sacred to the purposes of its organization, and cannot be lent to any one for any private purpose. He cannot be commissioned.

That such a person is willing to pay his own expenses to the field, and on it, does not alter the case. Even if he were by contribution to add largely to the means of the Commission, besides paying his own expenses, it would be giving the name and aid of the Commission in getting passes for private ends under color of a sacred public purpose.

Delegates when enlisted should be instructed specially to report themselves on the field to the field agent, and put themselves under his direction, and should stand pledged to do it. The Commission is greatly injured whenever delegates refuse to comply with our regulations and instructions, and perhaps most of all by those who *visit the various points of interest* as self-appointed inspectors or as curiosity seekers, instead of entering heartily into the work at such points as may be assigned to them.

INCIDENTS.

A few only can be given. They are selected without order as to time or place, and rather for variety of illustration than peculiar impressiveness. They will exhibit the work of the Commission in its processes and fruits in some of their many phases.

The first two following are given by Rev. Robert J. Parvin, of Cheltenham, and illustrate the work of delegates for both the

BODY AND SOUL.

"Charles C——, an orphan from Columbia County, New York, aged eighteen years, received a fatal wound from a ball passing through the upper part of his left lung. He lay for some two weeks in a barn belonging to the hospital of the Fifth Army Corps, and received there some little attention from us daily. Early in the morning of the day of his death, I said to him, 'Charley, the surgeon thinks that you cannot recover, and that you may not live a great while longer; is there anything you can think of which you would like to have me do for you, or any message which you would like to leave with me?' He turned his full blue eyes upon me, and said most earnestly, 'Oh! I must see my folks again! Can't I be taken home?' I answered, 'There is no possible thing for your comfort which we would not do for you, but you are not in a condition to be removed.' 'Pray for me,' was his next request. After praying for him, I said, 'Now, Charley, will you not look in simple trust to the precious Saviour, and pray for yourself?' With his eyes fixed upwards, and his hands clasped over his breast, he offered, in simple, touching terms, a prayer of dedication and supplication, in which his whole soul seemed to be deeply engaged. 'Lord Jesus, receive me.' 'I must come just as I am; Lord, pardon my sins, and save my soul?' 'Create in me a clean heart.' 'Make me thy child, and when I die, take me to heaven for Jesus' sake.' Such are a few of the petitions which in distinct tones he uttered. Soon afterward he fell into a quiet slumber, which lasted for over an hour. Awaking from it, he said, with a smile, 'I feel better now. . . . Tell uncle I am going home to die no more!' These were his last words on earth, for almost whilst yet the words trembled on his lips, his soul, as I believe, cleansed in the Saviour's blood, ascended to 'the home of the blessed,' 'to die no more.' "

A LITTLE HELP, JUST AT THE RIGHT TIME, OF GREAT VALUE, AND A SUBSEQUENT ACKNOWLEDGMENT A MOST ABUNDANT REWARD.

"Lieut. ——, of — Regiment, was shot through the lower part of the body. He was lying on the hard ground, and had been for several days, when I found him, having only his rubber blanket under him. I had in my trunk a bed-sack, made from a large sheet. I filled it with hay, and succeeded in getting him on it without causing him a great deal of pain. His sense of relief, and his thankfulness for it I cannot describe. Nourishment which we then prepared for him, he partook of and enjoyed, and his case and his feelings took a hopeful turn. A few days later, he was removed by ambulance and cars, still on his 'bed,' which he would not part with. Two weeks later I called on him at his own home in Philadelphia, and as I entered his room, with tearful eyes, his first words after a welcome were, addressing his wife, 'My dear, this is the gentleman I have told you of; he gave me that bed, and I believe he saved my life.' "

A LIFE SAVED.

Mr. James Grant, delegate, gives the following:

"When moving round amongst the wounded, who were lying scattered about the outside of the building used as an hospital by General Sedgwick's division, on the night after the Battle of Antietam, my attention was called by a wounded officer to a friend of his, whom he said was very badly wounded in the face, and was lying out somewhere without a covering.

"Directing me to the neighborhood where he was to be found, I started for the purpose, and throwing the rays of my lantern at the foot of a wooden fence, I soon discovered the object of my search.

"He was a Lieutenant in one of the Pennsylvania Regiments, and had during the battle been shot in the face. The ball had entered in at one side of the cheek, and passed out at the other, grazing his tongue, and carrying away several of his teeth. His face was horribly swollen, and as he could not move his jaw, he could not speak. On asking him if he was Lieutenant M——, of Philadelphia, he assented by a nod of his head. When I found him, he was reclining at the foot of a fence, and as it was raining pretty heavily, he was quite wet.

"Procuring a few bundles of straw, a bed was made for him, and after making him as comfortable as possible, he was left for the night. During the two following days his wound, which had been hurriedly dressed upon the field, had remained untouched. The surgeons were all very busy, and being of a very amiable disposition, he showed no signs of impatience. He had tasted no food, and it was pitiable to see him attempt to swallow even a mouthful of water. In the inflamed, wounded condition of his mouth, nothing could be passed down his throat.

"On the third day after our arrival here, as the surgeons had more to do than they could manage, we proceeded to assist them in washing and redressing the wounds of the men, most of which had remained untouched since the day of the battle. After some consideration, I took the Lieutenant's case in hand, and after about two hours' labor, succeeded in cutting away his whiskers, and washing the wound pretty thoroughly, both inside and outside the mouth. As soon as this was done, and all the clotted blood and matter cleared away, the swelling went down gradually, and he began to articulate a little. A day or so afterwards, he was able to swallow liquid, and being carefully cleaned and washed every day, in less than a week he was so far recovered as to be able to travel towards Philadelphia. The next time I saw him was in his own house, getting along wonderfully well. Tears of gratitude filled his own eyes, and those of his wife, and it amply repaid me for all the privations endured whilst working among the wounded of that bloody field, to be introduced to Mrs. M. by the gallant soldier, as 'the man who picked him up at midnight, and dressed his wound, when he had given himself up to die.' "

A PROTESTANT PROFESSOR PRAYING IN A CATHOLIC CHURCH, AT THE REQUEST OF A CATHOLIC LADY, FOR A DYING MAN.

"Rev. I. O. Sloan relates the following, to show how both political and religious differences are forgotten by those who love Jesus, in such scenes as those which follow a great battle.

"The Catholic Church, as well as others, was at first used as an hospital. The Sabbath after the battle, Professor Stoever was visiting the wounded brought to this church, as he did constantly wherever he could find sufferers to relieve. A brave boy, who had been laid in the chancel, was dying, and as Professor Stoever came down near him, a kind-hearted Catholic lady came to him, and said, 'Oh! I want you to go and talk and pray with that boy, for he is dying, and he is not converted.' He went and knelt by his side in the altar, thinking only of Christ and his pardoning grace, and prayed that God would be merciful, and forgive and bless that suffering, dying boy. Soon he died, and as we hope, leaning on the Saviour, and rejoicing in the faith of the righteous."

THE RIGHT DOCTOR.

Rev. B. B. Hotchkin, of Delaware county, Pennsylvania, gives, from Hagerstown, Maryland, under date of July 27th, the following touching incident:

"The first Sabbath after our arrival, and all the week succeeding, was filled up with the indispensable work of bodily relief, to save the lives of wounded men. There was no time nor opportunity for public worship, and our directly religious efforts were confined to labors at the bed-side, chiefly commending the dying to Christ.

"Yesterday (Sabbath) we proposed to the authorities of the Washington House Hospital, the largest in Hagerstown, to hold a public service with such of the patients as were able to be gathered into one company. The proposal was instantly acceded to, with what spirit you may judge from the reply of the surgeon, whose principal duty was in the large dining-room, then filled with four long rows of patients, all severe surgical cases. Said he, 'I have work here to keep me busy the whole day, but I will stop to give you time for worship any hour you wish. It will be good for the men.'

"The large door of the dining-room opened into the hotel office, which, with the hall, afforded room for all who were well enough to come down from the upper stories. A joyous thrill ran through the hospital, as the word went from story to story, and from room to room—'They are going to have preaching!' 'What is it? Are you going to have meeting?' said a patient in the dining-room to me, as he saw them bringing seats around the door. Being answered in the affirmative, he clasped his hands, and cried, Oh that is good! it is good! It is *so* long since I have had any such privilege!' He was a member of the Presbyterian Church in New Jersey, but in the army had long failed of falling in with the religious privileges which some camps and regiments afford. He had longed for them, and now to him this one day in the courts of the Lord was better than a thousand.

"I spoke to the audience of Christ, the Great Physician—the Physician whose exceeding excellency is, that his services are of surest and highest avail, when the skill of the earthly physician utterly fails. In the hands of the best surgeon they might die—some of them probably *must* die; but with the grace of the heavenly Physician, whose medicine is for the heart, they had the surety of everlasting life.

"To-day, passing along the dining-room, I heard a call, 'Preacher, preacher!' I went to the bed from which it came, and said to the sufferer, 'My poor friend, how do you feel?' 'Oh better, better,' said he, 'better, a great deal.' 'Do you feel like getting well?' 'Oh I don't know about that; but I have got the Doctor you told us about. He is my Doctor now; he has been with me all night; he is with me now, and I *am* better.' The sparkle of his eye, and glow of his face, spoke all that he meant. He may die, but I am persuaded he is better.

"Time fails me to add incidents. None know until they participate in this work, the value, the timeliness, and the blessedness of the Gospel preached amid such scenes, and to such assemblies. Preacher of God's comfort for the mourning, leave for a Sabbath or two your frescoed church and your draperied pulpit, and try the power of the word of salvation among the dying victims of war, and you will believe what I say."

A REBEL PENITENT.

"Oh for a gift to speak of the great good the Christian Commission is doing! Oh that the good people that give could see how much they do! I have just left the bedside of a rebel, who was reading a little Christian book, and crying. Through his tears he said to me, 'The good Christian Association gave this book to me, and this cooling drink, and these preserved peaches. But, Oh, better than this, they have led me to the Saviour; and now, if I can hop on one foot into heaven, I will not regret the loss of my leg. If only through it I have found my heavenly Father, I shall be more than satisfied. Go and see Mr. Stuart, and give him the thanks of a rebel penitent.'

"Rev. George F. Willis."

MOTHER AND SON ON THE BATTLE-FIELD.

Mr. John Wiest, in a very interesting account of work done on the battle-field of Gettysburg, gives the following incident:

"On Saturday, Adjutant J. J. Blinn observed a woman in a tent near his own, when he exclaimed, 'My mother! my mother!' On Wednesday his mother was telegraphed to come on and see her son before he died. I was in this lovely young man's tent when his mother arrived. The scene was most touching and affecting. Weak and exhausted, he told his mother that those around him were his friends, to which

I added, that her dear son had not only those around him as friends, but Christ Jesus, the best of all friends, was also his friend. With tears of joy, Mrs. Blinn rejoined, 'Then your mother can willingly see her son die.' This noble and brave young man left home out of Christ, became a Christian in his country's service, and died a most happy death. Such triumphs of the glorious Gospel may well encourage the, at times, disheartened laborer in the vineyard of Christ. Very few of the men, yes, very few indeed, are indifferent to their spiritual interests."

TAKING THE BITTER OUT OF THE WAR.

Mr. Joseph Ward, delegate, relates the following: "Our work for many days was almost entirely for the bodies of the men, but from time to time occasion was found to speak a word to the soul. At one time ten men were brought from a barn, a few miles from town, where they had been lying since the battle of Falling Waters, more than ten days, with little or no care. One of them was an old man, apparently just ready to die from exhaustion and fatigue. He had only strength to say, 'So sick, so sick; tired.' After I had washed his face and hands, and bathed his head, I gave him a little tea (he was too weak to take more than one swallow without resting,) which revived him a little, so that he said, 'God bless you! and God *will* bless you; I know He will.' After giving him time to sleep, I washed him and put on clean clothes, when his gratitude seemed boundless. 'Oh! I am a new man; but I don't understand it. Are you a surgeon?' 'No.' 'Are you a ward-master!' 'No.' 'Do you live in this town?' 'No.' 'Well, who are you?' 'An agent of the Christian Commission.' 'Oh! I might have known that if I had thought a moment. They are doing a great deal of good, and taking a great deal of the bitter out of this war.' He improved every day, and when I left him was able to walk all about the camp.

"A part of our work was among the rebels, one hundred and twenty of them being in the Seminary Hospital, and after the men were moved to tents, they were in the same camp with us. They received our aid thankfully in most cases. Among others there was a Colonel of a Georgia regiment, who made special inquiry concerning the work of the Commission, and mourned that they had nothing of the kind at the South. When I left the camp, one of their officers came to our tent, and bade me goodbye, and thanked me in their name for the work of the Commission."

AN IMPRESSIVE SERVICE.

The following is the closing paragraph of the report of Rev. George W. Shinn:

"Perhaps the most impressive service I ever attended, was held on Sunday evening last, in the square between the tents. It was a beautiful evening. The sun's rays had hardly disappeared, and the moon had risen. A few clouds were off in the west, and occasionally flashes of lightning would dart from one to another. The camp was in a beautiful field of clover, and the rows of white tents stretched along the four sides of the field. In full view was the Round Top Mountain, the scene of the desperate struggle of three weeks ago.

"There were three army chaplains and three clergymen of us on the ground, besides the laymen of the Commission. Most of the attendants, ladies, and the other well persons on the ground, assembled, and the service began by singing a hymn. The music drew together as many of the wounded as could hobble about, and others who were able to do so turned over on their couches to listen. Prayer was offered, and addresses were made, interspersed with the singing of hymns. Nothing could have been more interesting or affecting than this scene. I shall never forget it. I felt it my duty to tell the men that it seemed to me to be highly probable they would never be placed in any situation where it would be so easy to become Christians as there, and and at that time. The gates of the eternal world seemed swung wide open. The air seemed continually bearing along upon it the name of the Saviour. Hymns of praise to Him—cries for mercy to Him—words of trust upon Him—were continually uttered.

"It has never been my privilege to see such a large body of men so much interested in religion as the men of Corps No. 2 are now. Some clergymen should be continually on the ground to satisfy the craving of souls for the bread of life.

"I shall ever remember the past week as one of the best I have ever spent."

"THAT IS CHRISTIANITY."

The following striking incidents are from the report of Rev. W. D. Siegfried, one of the numerous workers on the memorable battle-field of Pennsylvania:

"A young man from Wisconsin, badly wounded, after receiving food and drink, and such delicacies as he seemed to need, from my hand, wept tears of gratitude, and inquired, 'What is the Christian Commission intended for,—only for soldiers? How do they afford all these things they give us?' Several of his fellow-soldiers turned eagerly towards me, as I proceeded to answer the question, they evidently feeling interested in it. After assuring him that the Commission work was prosecuted entirely through Christian benevolence, he remarked, 'Well, that *is* Christianity—that *is* religion! I shall never forget the Christian Commission delegates at Gettysburg.' Several voices responded, 'Neither will I.'"

"NO RED TAPE HERE."

"A brave young man, not seriously wounded, came limping up to our tent, and requested some cloths and other articles to dress his wound, himself, as all hands were busy with worse cases. The articles I handed him at once, at the same time giving him a drink of ice-cold lemonade just prepared. 'Ah!' said he, 'there's no red tape process here! You men of the Christian Commission give a fellow what he needs, when he needs it, without a tedious process of waiting for orders, and then waiting for them to be filled. Thank you, gentlemen.' And he turned away with a glad heart."

EXAMPLE OF DELEGATE WORK ON THE BATTLE-FIELD.

Rev. J. E. Adams, of Maine, writes, under date of July 29th, 1863:

"We were the first on the ground of the 3d Division, 2d Corps Hospital, Gettysburg, both with delegates and supplies. Two delegates were there Saturday, Mr. Cook from Baltimore, and Mr. Stittson of Rochester, New York. Several others arrived Sabbath morning after the battle. We at once gave ourselves to the work of distributing cordials and bread and clothing to the wounded and dying. We gave them water, bound up their wounds, made them as comfortable as was possible under the circumstances, and in all this ministering to the *bodily* wants of these poor men, we pointed their *souls* to Christ, and urged them to seek pardon for their sins, and consecrate themselves to God and his service. On Monday the cry was 'Bread! bread!' Fortunately, one of our delegates found some good farmers at the town with a load of nice loaves, and after our case was stated they drove into camp with it, and gave it into our hands for distribution. How grateful the hungry boys were! 'God bless you!' 'God bless the Christian Commission!' 'This is like home!' 'Oh, how good!' rang out continually as we passed along. Thus our work continued for days, feeding the hungry, clothing the naked, giving drink to the thirsting, binding up the wounds, and changing the position of the suffering, breathing consolation to the disheartened and the dying. None but those who witnessed this can appreciate the gratitude of the soldiers, and realize the good that was done. No doubt many valuable lives were saved."

ARMY CONVERSIONS.

Rev. J. L. Heysinger, delegate, mentions the following:

"J. B. Church, 47th New York. Badly wounded. Doubtful case. Says he was converted to God about a year ago in camp, through the agency of T. O. Crawford, of the Christian Commission. G. H. Hawes, 7th Wisconsin, converted at the station of the Christian Commission, Belle Plain. Wrote a letter to his mother full of hope."

AN OHIO SOLDIER.

Rev. Geo. H Morss, in his report says:

"A soldier from an Ohio regiment was suffering from a very painful wound in the knee by a shell. I approached his bed and said to him, 'My friend, how do you feel to-day?' 'Oh, I am rather poorly to-day,' he said; 'but sometimes I am more cheerful,' and he beckoned for me to come around to the other side of his bed. I did so, when he said he wanted to sit up and see if he wouldn't feel better. I carefully raised him up, and after sitting a little while, he called for his nurse to help lay him back again. Together we carefully lowered him upon his pillow; still he suffered much pain and cried out from its severity. I stood by him trying to cheer and comfort him, when feeling that he needed quiet rest, I said to him, 'I will leave you now, for you need rest, and I am afraid I shall weary you by talking.' 'O no,' said he; 'don't leave me, don't leave me; stay here,' and he caught hold of my coat and pulled me closer to his side. 'Oh, well, said I, if you wish me to stay, certainly I will stay with you,' and I stooped down over him and began to talk to him of Jesus, the blessed Comforter, the Man of Sorrows, acquainted with grief, who was willing to be near all his sorrowing, suffering children, to help them bear their griefs. 'Oh!' said he 'how good it is to have some one to talk to me so now.' 'Then you love the name of Jesus, do you?' said I. 'Yes, he is my strength and support now; I could not do without him.' 'When did you first find Jesus a Saviour." 'On the battle-field, sir.' 'How was that?' I asked. 'Why, I had heard much of Jesus, and I determined to know myself if he was such a Saviour as I had heard he was. I sought him on the battle-field and found him, and he has been a precious Saviour to me since.'"

INFORMATION AND INSTRUCTION ABOUT STORES.

All good and suitable stores are welcomed, and all necessary freight and charges paid on them by the Commission, and are distributed by delegates of the Christian Commission personally.

WHAT TO SEND.

Money, by all means, if possible. To invest money in articles to send is unwise.

The Commission can purchase exactly what is wanted, at the very moment when needed most, and as a Commission at wholesale cheaper than others.

CLOTHING, ETC.

Cotton shirts,
Cotton drawers,
Canton flannel shirt sand drawers,
Surgical shirts and drawers, with tape strings to tie instead of seams at the sides,)
Large cotton drawers, (to wear in-doors as pants,)
Dressing gowns,
Slippers, (if of cloth or carpet, with stiff soles,)
Sheets,
Pillow-cases,
Bed-ticks, (single for filling with straw,)
Pillows,
Pads, for fractured limbs,
Ring pads, for wounds,
Fans,
Netting, to protect from flies,
Housewifes, stored with needles, thread, buttons, and pins, &c.,
Handkerchiefs,
Wash-rags,
Old linen.

FOOD, ETC.

Oat meal,
Farina,
Corn starch,
Dried rusk,
Jellies,
Soda biscuit,
Butter crackers,
Boston crackers,
Pickles,
Jams,
Onions, in barrels,
Apples, in barrels,
Cranberries,
Good butter, in small jars,
Dried fruits.

In special cases, eggs, bread, cakes, &c., are needed, but not generally. They should never be sent unless specially called for.

FOR BEVERAGES.

Good black tea, Chocolate, Lemons, Syrups.

All preparations of the blackberry are of double value.

STIMULANTS.

Good brandy, Madeira wine, Port wine, Cordials.

Domestic wines are excellent in winter, apt to spoil in summer.

Good Reading Matter.—Send no trash. Soldiers deserve the best. A library is a valuable hygienic appliance. For the able-bodied, good publications are mental and spiritual food. For convalescents, lively, interesting books, the monthlies, the pictorials, works of art, science, and literature, as well as those for moral and spiritual culture, such as you would put into the hands of a brother recovering.

Stationery is much needed, paper, envelopes, and pencils.

HOW TO PACK.

Pack in boxes. Barrels are not as good. Secure well. Boxes should not be so large that two cannot conveniently lift them into a wagon. Pack eatables by themselves. Never pack perishable articles, such as oranges, lemons, bread, cakes, nor jars of jellies and jams, with other goods. Tin cans should be soldered; all other modes fail. Stone jars should be corked and firmly bound with oiled linen or leather over the cork, and packed closely in sawdust or hay, in boxes never exceeding a dozen and a half in a box, and nailed strongly, to bear rough handling. Jellies in tumblers, covered with paper, and wines, cordials, &c., in bottles, with paper or other poor stoppers, are liable to spill out, and if packed with other things, sure to injure them.

HOW TO MARK.

Mark with paint or ink on the boards,—cards rub off,—in plain letters and figures. On one corner, the number of the box according to the number sent by you in all, numbering your first box *1, your second *2, your third *3, and so on from the first sent to the last. On another corner, mark each box as from your Society, giving the name, and conspicuously also mark as follows:

"George H. Stuart,
Chairman Christian Commission,
11 Bank Street, Philadelphia,"

or whatever other name and place you wish to send it to.

To secure acknowledgments, and to save trouble, also send an invoice or list by mail, on paper, the common letter-sheet size, written only on one side, specifying each box or barrel by number, and giving the contents of each by itself. Give your own name and post-office in full, with the name of your State. Place also another list or invoice of the same kind in the box under the lid, and if with this last you place also an envelope addressed to yourself, with a postage stamp upon it, you may sometimes,—not always,—have it returned to you through the mail, with the signature of the delegate, and the name of the hospital camp where he distributed it.

Write plain. Above all, write your own name distinctly, and to save embarrassment, give your address in full, especially whether Miss or Mrs. or Rev.

Money should be sent to Joseph Patterson, Esq., Treasurer, at Western Bank, Philadelphia.

LADIES' CHRISTIAN COMMISSION OF ——.

PREAMBLE.

Whereas, Vast numbers of the men of our country have entered the national service to put down the rebellion and save the Union, and have left homes and churches, with all their comforts and privileges, and are subject to the perils, hardships, and deprivations of battles, marches, and of life in the camp, if well, or in the hospital if wounded or sick;

And whereas, In the good providence of God the United States Christian Commission for the Army and Navy has been formed, as an electric chain between the hearth and the tent, to promote the temporal and spiritual interests of the men in the service, and invites the aid of ladies in this patriotic and holy work;

And whereas, Ladies cannot themselves take up arms in defence of the Union, but can aid in benefiting those who are in arms for this hallowed cause;

Therefore we, loyal ladies of America, do associate ourselves together for this purpose as

THE LADIES' CHRISTIAN COMMISSION OF ——,

AUXILIARY TO THE UNITED STATES CHRISTIAN COMMISSION,

For the Army and Navy,

and for our better regulation and government do adopt the following

CONSTITUTION.

ARTICLE 1. The object of this society shall be to aid the United States Christian Commission in all suitable ways in its work of benefiting the men of our army and navy temporally and spiritually.

ART. 2. Any lady, by vote of the Board of Managers, may become a member of this society upon the payment of —— monthly. Any gentleman may, by vote of the Managers, become an associate member by the monthly payment of ——. Any lady or gentleman may, by vote of the Board of Managers, become an honorary member of the Commission upon the payment of ——, or a life member upon the payment of ——.

ART. 3. The affairs of the society shall be conducted by a Board of Managers, consisting of —— members, who shall hold office one year from ——, or until others are elected to fill their place, and who shall elect from their own number a President, —— Vice Presidents, a Secretary, and a Treasurer.

ART. 4. It shall be the duty of the President to preside in all meetings, both of the Commission and of the Board of Managers, and see that the regulations adopted are observed, and its plans and purposes are promptly and effectively carried out.

The Vice-Presidents shall aid the President as circumstances may require; and in the absence of the President from any meeting of the Commission or Board of Managers, some one of the Vice-Presidents shall preside.

The Secretary shall conduct the general correspondence of the Commission, and keep a record of all its proceedings, and render monthly reports of the same to the Board of Managers.

The Treasurer shall take charge of the money received by the Commission, keep it safely, and pay it out, from time to time, upon the order of the President on behalf of the Board of Managers, keep an account of all moneys received and paid out, make public acknowledgment from time to time of that which is received, and render account from time to time of all receipts and disbursements as the Board of Managers may require.

The Board of Managers shall have the general control of all the affairs of the Commission. ——— shall be a quorum for the transaction of business. They shall fill vacancies in their own Board, elect an Executive Committee consisting of ——— of their own members, ——— of whom shall be a quorum for business; elect committees to carry out their various objects, pass such by-laws as may be deemed necessary, and appoint agents or delegates to act for them in the collection of money or the transaction of any business committed to them, and render a full report to the Commission at its annual meeting.

Art. 5. All moneys received by this Commission, over and above what may be required for the purchase of materials for clothing, and pay such expenses as may be necessarily incurred, shall from time to time be transmitted, by order of the Board of Managers, to the Treasurer of the United States Christian Commission, (or of ——— ——— Branch of the United States Christian Commission,) in aid of its work.

Art. 6. The Commission shall hold a meeting annually, at which time the Board of Managers shall be elected by ballot, each member casting one vote. And the President, by order of the Board of Managers, may call meetings of the Commission at such other times as occasion may require.

The Board of Managers shall meet as frequently as once in each month, at such time and place as they may appoint.

And the Executive Committee shall meet once a week, on such day as may be agreed upon by them.

www.ingramcontent.com/pod-product-compliance
Lightning Source LLC
LaVergne TN
LVHW011122110826
845150LV00008B/2222

* 9 7 8 1 4 1 8 1 9 5 3 2 8 *